POCKET
ENCOURAGER
for *Young Adults*

POCKET ENCOURAGER

for Young Adults

Biblical Help for Difficult Times

By Selwyn Hughes
with contributions from
Dr Bill and Frances Munro
Hilary Vogel • David and Maureen Brown
Keith Tondeur • Helena Wilkinson

*May our
Lord Jesus Christ himself
and God our Father,
who loved us and by his grace
gave us eternal encouragement
and good hope,
encourage your hearts
and strengthen you
in every good deed and word.*

2 Thessalonians 2:16–17

Pocket Encourager for Young Adults

Copyright © CWR 2001
Reprinted 2001
ISBN 1 85345 180 0

Concept development, editing, design and production by CWR

Printed in England by Linney Print

Published by CWR, Waverley Abbey House, Waverley Lane,
Farnham, Surrey GU9 8EP

Contents

Everyone needs
Encouragement

*E*very one of us needs to be encouraged. As a counsellor I have met only a few people who didn't respond well to a few carefully chosen, biblically-based words of support. Some of the most memorable moments in my own life have been when I've been stressed by a problem and someone has come and stimulated my faith with a God-given word of reassurance.

The word discourage means "to deprive of courage, to dishearten, to deter". We often face discouraging situations; a put-down from someone, plans that don't work out, loneliness, failure or doubts. The word encourage means "to inspire with new confidence and courage, to give spirit or hope, to hearten, to spur on, to give help." It is gratifying when we are caught up in discouragement to have someone come alongside and say something (or do something) that is encouraging. But what do we do when such a friend isn't available?

That famous Old Testament character David was in this kind of situation in the First Book of Samuel chapters 27, 29 and 30. Fleeing for his life from King Saul, David offered his services, and those of his 600 men, to King Achish, a Philistine. The king accepted, giving David and his men first Gath, then the city of

Ziklag for their home. David, his men and their families settled there.

One day King Achish took his troops to join in a combined Philistine attack against Israel. Astonishingly David and his soldiers went along with them to fight against their own people. But King Achish's colleagues refused to trust David and his men in a battle against their own so they decided to send them back to Ziklag. On returning there they found that a group of desert raiders called the Amalekites had burned the city to the ground and had taken captive everyone they had found. David and his men "wept aloud until they had no strength left to weep" (1 Samuel 30:4).

David's men turned on him and blamed him for their predicament and even discussed stoning him: "each one was bitter in spirit because of his sons and daughters" (1 Samuel 30:6). In addition to these problems David also had to cope with the loss of his own family. His state of distress was such that right there his career could easily have come to an end. Then we are introduced to one of the great "buts" of the Bible: "But David encouraged ... himself in the Lord his God" (v.6, Amplified Bible).

How did he do it? He would have prayed of course, and that is always important when dealing with discouragement. But I think he did something more – he recalled what he knew of God, and thought about what he had learned concerning the Almighty as a shepherd boy when he meditated upon

Him in the Judean hills.

"The secret of recovering your footing spiritually," says Jim Packer, the well-known theologian, "lies in the little word think." That was undoubtedly where David began; he made himself recall what he knew of God and applied it to his own situation at that moment. The Puritans used to call it "preaching to oneself". Every time we reel under the blow of some traumatic experience, every time our feelings scream out in pain, we must assert the facts of our faith over our feelings. We can't wait for the unpleasant and uncomfortable feelings to subside; we must take control over the runaway feelings by reminding ourselves of what we know about God.

I imagine that David would have reminded himself that God is sovereign, God is love, God is forgiving, God is faithful, God is consistent, God is merciful. Dwelling on these thoughts would have brought great encouragement to David's heart. The consequence of all this was that he found the guidance he needed to restore the situation completely. Read the story for yourself in the rest of 1 Samuel 30.

Every young Christian man or woman ought to know how to do what David did, and this pocketbook is an attempt to help you in doing that. Friends are great (thank God for them), but we must know how to think biblically about life's problems, to talk to ourselves about the facts of our faith and then find the appropriate scriptures that relate to our problem. It's essential to know what parts of the Bible to turn to and to know how to talk ourselves into a new mood of optimism and faith. The things we tell ourselves greatly affect the way we feel. Negative self-talk is often responsible for the way we feel. We talk ourselves into a low mood by telling ourselves things that either minimise or maximise the facts. Just as we talk ourselves into downcast feelings so we can talk ourselves out of them.

In this publication we have taken key issues addressed in the earlier CWR publication *Your Personal Encourager,* and added other material relevant to young adults. If a particular problem that you face doesn't fall within these categories then look for the one that comes closest to it. I feel confident you will find something that will revive, refresh and minister to your spirit. Use this book to help you find a relevant scripture and thoughts to confront your discouragement and also as a tool for ministering to others.

The power of this publication lies in the Scripture which it highlights. I have also given some explanations and statements of my own together with a prayer that can be used at the end. In every instance prayer is vital and should be based on Scripture and built around such great themes as God's sovereignty, power, compassion, forgiveness – the same truths that David would have reflected on in those discouraging moments at Ziklag. The thoughts and ideas recorded here have been used in countless counselling situations over the years. Many people have told me they have found them helpful. I hope you will too.

One final thing, encouragement is not mere sentimentality. Scripture is equally encouraging when it confronts and challenges us as it is when it consoles and comforts us. To be faced with a challenge when we are hurting may not be what we most want, but it may be what we most need. An African tribe describes medicine that tastes bad but does them good as "It hurts better." Realise that when God challenges us it is only so that we might be brought to the place of complete and utter dependency upon Him. God not only lifts the standards to great heights, but also provides the power to reach up to them.

Personally, I find it deeply encouraging that God thinks so much of me that He will not let me get away with things that damage my potential and hinder my effectiveness for Him. *He loves me as I am but He loves me too much to let me stay as I am*. So remember it is still the ministry of encouragement that is at work when Scripture speaks to us in a challenging and confronting way.

May you, like David, learn the skill of encouraging yourself and others in the Lord your God.

Selwyn Hughes

Selwyn Hughes,
Waverley Abbey House, Farnham, Surrey, England.

POCKET ENCOURAGER

for Young Adults

When Betrayed by a
Friend

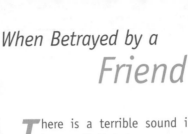

*T*here is a terrible sound in the word "betrayed". To betray someone is to deal treacherously with them. In a hard and cruel world such as this we are not surprised when we are hurt by our enemies, but no one expects to be hurt by a friend. Few things, I imagine, would have hurt our Lord more than to be betrayed by one of His own disciples. How do we cope with betrayal?

First, we must take our pain to God and invite Him to invade our hearts with His soothing balm. All painful situations must be faced, even though they do not have to be dwelt upon. We must let God minister to us in our hurt; He is the only One who can "restore the soul".

Because hurt can quickly escalate into resentment, we must also empty our heart of all bitterness and – forgive (with the help of the Lord). Forgiveness, it must be understood, may not always bring about changes in the other person (nor guarantee that he or she will want to be restored), but it will ensure release for our own soul.

The cross of our Lord Jesus Christ stands and holds out wide appealing arms to all who have been betrayed. It says: "This is how Jesus dealt with His enemies ... and the friend who betrayed Him." In the light of that great fact can we do anything other than forgive?

"When you forgive, you in no way change the past – but you sure do change the future."

Bernard Meltzer

Suggested further reading
1 Peter 3:8–12

Reflect and respond
Are you harbouring any pain?

Have you forgiven the person who has wronged you?

Ask the Father to give you healing grace.

When You Know You're Being
Selfish

*T*he root cause of most of our problems,
is to be found in selfishness and self-
centredness. Who hasn't been astonished in
moments of honest self-examination to
discover how much of what we do has a
self-reference? Isn't our instinctive
reaction to the things that happen around
us to say to ourselves: "How will this
affect me?" Selfishness and self-centredness is so natural to us that it is only
when we make ourselves face it that the
full horror of it comes home.

There is little we can do to correct this
distortion of our nature by ourselves, and
this is why we must turn to Christ for help.
Our Lord's first thoughts were never of
Himself, and He alone can help us love as
He loved. When we read the Gospels we do
not find one occasion for which our Lord
could be convicted of selfishness. Even when
facing crucifixion His thoughts were of
forgiveness for those who were crucifying Him.
He saved Peter, three-times-denying Peter, by a

look, and paused to say to the women who lined the path to Calvary: "Do not weep for me; weep for yourselves and for your children" (Luke 23:28).

Selfishness arises out of insecurity – the feeling that we have nothing to give away. Only a close, deep and ongoing relationship with Christ can overwhelm our natural self-interest and move us from self-centredness to other-centredness.

"Are people seeing that you are a Christian or are they seeing Christ in you?"

Ulf Ekman

Bible Verses to Help You

Be imitators of God, therefore, as dearly loved children and live a life of love, just as Christ loved us and gave himself up for us as a fragrant offering and sacrifice to God.
(Ephesians 5:1–2)

But I am among you as one who serves. *(Luke 22:27)*

Suggested further reading
Philippians 2:1–11

Reflect and respond
Self-giving is the hallmark of Christianity – commit to be self-less.

Meditate on Christ's example as described in Ephesians 5:2

When You're Afraid of *Death*

Christian studies on the subject of death
show three underlying concerns: the
physical fact of dying, the fear of finality,
the fear of judgment. Not all three
elements are always present, and one or
two elements may be stronger in some
than others.

People fear the physical fact of dying
because of the possibility of great pain,
but the beneficent power of modern drugs
makes the chances of this remote. A
number of thanatologists (people who
conduct research into the stages of dying)
say that the struggle some people demon-
strate in death is largely unconscious, and
is more agonising for those looking on than
for the person concerned.

The second fear – the fear of finality –
need not concern a Christian. Death does not
end all. The resurrection of our Lord proves
that the spiritual part of us survives death,
and that it was death that died, not He.

The third fear – the fear of judgment – is not

as strong as it once was in human minds. This is due in no small measure to the fact that fewer people attend church, and that teaching on the final judgment seems in some churches (not all) to be non-existent. No man or woman who knows Christ need fear judgment. God has consumed our sin and incinerated it at Calvary. Our Lord stands as a great wall between penitent sinners and their sin. We simply must rejoice in that other things may perish but a Christian never.

"When the devil reminds you of your problems, you remind him of his defeat."

Gabriel Heymans

Bible Verses to Help You

"Where, O death, is your victory? Where, O death, is your sting?" The sting of death is sin, and the power of sin is the law. But thanks be to God! He gives us the victory through our Lord Jesus Christ. *(1 Corinthians 15:55–57)*

... as in Adam all die, so in Christ all will be made alive. *(1 Corinthians 15:22)*

Suggested further reading

Psalm 23

Reflect and respond

Allow this scripture to infuse your being:

"I give them eternal life, and they shall never perish; no-one can snatch them out of my hand." (John 10:28)

When Troubled by
Temptation

*T*emptation can be extremely harassing, yet we ought not to think of it as something entirely negative. The Greek word *"peirasmos"* means to test, to try, or to prove. There is no question of entrapment or seduction on the part of God in allowing us to be tempted; He permits it to come in order to strengthen us and equip us for more effective service in His kingdom. When Jesus went into the wilderness it was said that He went in "full of the Holy Spirit" (Luke 4:1), but He came out "in the power of the Spirit" (Luke 4:14). Mere fullness had turned to power under the pressure of temptation. No matter how strong and fierce the temptations that beset us, we have the firm promise in Scripture that God will engineer a way of escape.

Paul put it in 1 Corinthians 10:13: "God is faithful; he will not let you be tempted beyond what you can bear ... he will also provide a way out so that you can stand up under it."

How does the Almighty provide us with a way

of escape when harassed by oppressive temptations? He does it by infusing us with the strength and power to resist. There will never be a moment in our lives when God's grace and empowerment are unable to match (and surpass) the power of temptation. This means there is always, *always*, a way out.

Flee temptation and don't leave a forwarding address.

Bible Verses to Help You

No temptation has seized you except what is common to man. And God is faithful; he will not let you be tempted beyond what you can bear. But when you are tempted, he will also provide a way out so that you can stand up under it. *(1 Corinthians 10:13)*

Because he himself suffered when he was tempted, he is able to help those who are being tempted. *(Hebrews 2:18)*

Suggested further reading

James 1:13–15

Reflect and respond

"Watch and pray so that you will not fall into temptation. The spirit is willing, but the body is weak." (Matthew 26:41)

It is wise at times to simply run from temptation's grasp.

Remember, it's God who provides the way out and the strength to take it.

When Having Problems with
Jealousy

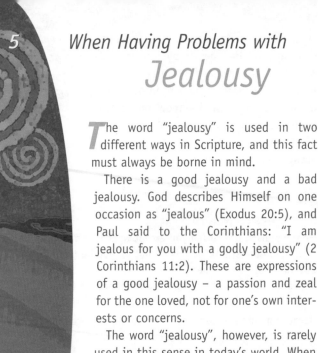

*T*he word "jealousy" is used in two different ways in Scripture, and this fact must always be borne in mind.

There is a good jealousy and a bad jealousy. God describes Himself on one occasion as "jealous" (Exodus 20:5), and Paul said to the Corinthians: "I am jealous for you with a godly jealousy" (2 Corinthians 11:2). These are expressions of a good jealousy – a passion and zeal for the one loved, not for one's own interests or concerns.

The word "jealousy", however, is rarely used in this sense in today's world. When we speak of "jealousy" we usually mean bad jealousy exhibited by feelings of coldness and resentment when others against whom we match ourselves in thought, appearance or accomplishment are praised and commended. Jealousy is not normally directed against those who are far above us in attainment; it is focused on those in our immediate circle, those on a par with ourselves or inferior to ourselves. *Jealousy is rooted in a wrong comparison with others*.

Comparing ourselves with others can swiftly lead to sin. If we feel another is not as good as us we can fall prey to pride; if we feel he or she is better than us we are tempted to imply they are hypocrites; if they are more successful than us we often slide into envy.

Jealousy can be dealt with only by keeping our eyes firmly fixed on Jesus and by comparing ourselves with Him alone.

Love is blind; jealousy sees too much.

Jewish Proverb

Bible Verses to Help You

A heart at peace gives life to the body, but envy rots the bones. *(Proverbs 14:30)*

My eyes are ever on the Lord, for only he will release my feet from the snare. *(Psalm 25:15)*

Suggested further reading

2 Corinthians 10:12–18

Reflect and respond

Have you fallen into the trap of comparing yourself with others?

Turn your eyes from others and fix your eyes on Jesus.

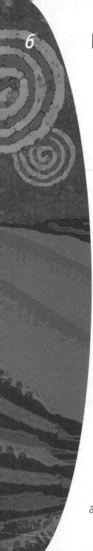

When Fighting
Discouragement

Whenever we feel discouraged, we have a battle on our hands. You do not have to fight the battle alone. Indeed, if you attempt to do so you will be overpowered.

Whatever our battle, spiritual, emotional or even physical, we need to put on the armour of God. In Ephesians 6 Paul lists six pieces of armour worn by the Roman soldiers: helmet, breastplate, belt, shoes, shield and the sword.

For the soldier in battle, the helmet protected the brain. One of our most vulnerable parts is the mind, listening to the enemy's lies. The breastplate is the covering of Christ's righteousness, by which alone we are acceptable to God. The belt had to be well-fitting or else the soldier could not walk freely, and we need to keep the truth of God's Word close to us all the time. The shield covered the whole body and it was vital in battle. Our shield is our faith, but we need to use it for protection. We also need to use the sword, the Word of God, to speak over ourselves the words which God speaks. And as we walk around in our armour we mustn't forget that we walk with our feet fitted with peace.

Take up your defence every day, otherwise you weaken your position. Soldiers put on their armour to prepare for battle. We need to do the same. Paul also tells us to "pray in the Spirit on all occasions with all kinds of prayers and requests".

You're in a battle – make sure you are equipped with the armour to win.

"Never doubt in the dark what God told you in the light."
Victor Raymond Edman

Bible Verses to Help You

"... fight the good fight, holding on to faith ... ."
(1 Timothy 1:18)

To you, O Lord, I lift up my soul; in you I trust, O my God. Do not let me be put to shame, nor let my enemies triumph over me. No-one whose hope is in you will ever be put to shame ... *(Psalm 25:1–3)*

Suggested further reading

1 Peter 1:6–7

Reflect and respond

You are in a battle! – put on the armour of God every day. Pray on all occasions, as though in a battle. Declare victory. Use the Word of God to cut down the enemy.

When God Doesn't Seem to be *There*

"**W**here is God in my situation?" you may ask. "It is difficult to pray, I don't know if God can hear me". Yes He can hear and He does want to hear you. Your prayers matter to Him. He knows the situation anyway, but He loves to hear your voice. Like a parent who listens for his/her child's voice, so God listens for you.

The Lord's Prayer begins, "Our Father" and so the foundation of prayer is that God is our Father. It then moves on to, "Hallowed be Thy name". Hallow comes from the Greek *Hagiazo*, which means to make holy, to sanctify.

If we do not begin our prayer with praise, but by praying about our problem, all we see is our problem. When we begin by praising God and lifting His name up, it puts life into perspective. Out of that place of praise it is easier to come to God and ask Him for your needs to be met.

Surrender precedes request. If we are not surrendered to God and walking with Him as

Lord of our life, we are not in a position to ask. It is easy to blame God, "You haven't answered". But there is a responsibility on our part first to surrender. Make sure that no sin comes between you and God. Sin is a separator.

Having checked your motives and spiritual health, you are left with one final detail – trust your Heavenly Father!

"God always answers us in the deeps, never in the shallows of our soul."

Amy Carmichael

Bible Verses to Help You

"... his ears are attentive to their prayer ... ." *(1 Peter 3:12)*

For the sake of his great name the Lord will not reject his people, because the Lord was pleased to make you his own. *(1 Samuel 12:22)*

Suggested further reading

Isaiah 49:15–16

Reflect and respond

God loves to hear your voice – talk to Him!

Begin your prayer by praising God.

Listen to what God has to say to you.

When You Get the
Blame

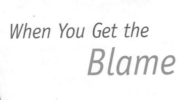

We live in a culture of blame. Always the cry is Whose fault is it? Who was to blame? Who should be punished? Graffiti on a Chicago subway stated, Humpty Dumpty was pushed. Manufacturers and accident insurers in the USA are so afraid of being sued, that they go to extreme lengths to try to protect themselves. The cry is, Someone should pay for this.

Studies have shown that the more a victim blames another person for the accident, the more poorly he copes. Anger and bitterness can go on for years. Being unforgiving, angry, resentful and bitter is wrong in God's eyes, but it can also damage our minds and bodies and delay recovery. We teach to forgive and not to harbour bitterness. "Get rid of all bitterness, rage and anger, brawling and slander, along with every form of malice. Be kind and compassionate to one another, forgiving each other, just as in Christ God forgave you"

(Ephesians 4:31–32). It may be difficult, almost impossible to do in our own strength, and often we will need God's help and grace to do it, but do it we must if we do not want to be damaged ourselves.

Deal with the faults of others as gently as with your own.

Chinese Proverb

Even more important, we must forgive so that we may be forgiven. "And when you stand praying, if you hold anything against anyone, forgive him, so that your Father in heaven may forgive you your sins" (Mark 11:25).

Bible Verses to Help You

Resentment kills a fool ... *(Job 5:2)*

Be kind and compassionate to one another, forgiving each other, just as in Christ God forgave you. *(Ephesians 4:32)*

Suggested further reading

Colossians 3:1–15; 1 Corinthians 13:5

Reflect and respond

Are you harbouring resentment or a grudge?

Is there someone you need to forgive?

Love keeps no record of wrongs – look to put right any wrongs this week.

When Plagued by Feelings of
Inferiority

*F*requently one hears the term "inferiority complex" bandied about. It is often used to describe the low sense of worth many young people carry around with them, usually the consequence of ineffective parenting. A low sense of worth may blight a whole life and at its worst can develop into self-rejection, even hate. Most young people learn how to cope with the problem by keeping away from situations in which they might be shown up as inferior, and thus live their lives at a lower level than God intends.

Whatever forces have gone into shaping our thoughts and ideas about ourselves (and we must be careful not to hold bitterness or resentment against those who nurtured us), we who are Christians must stand before God and draw the estimate of ourselves from Him. However little worth there may be in our nature, God put worth upon us by dying for our salvation. No one is to be despised (not even by him or herself) when they were dear enough to God that He shed His sacred blood. That is the ground of our worth, the solid, sufficient and only basis for it. And it is the same for everyone.

This last statement must be allowed to soak into our minds, for it is only when we see that worth is not something that is earned but something bestowed that self-despising can be rooted out of our minds.

"What other people think of me is becoming less and less important; what they think of Jesus because of me is critical."

Cliff Richard

Bible Verses to Help You

Therefore, there is now no condemnation for those who are in Christ Jesus ... *(Romans 8:1)*

So you are no longer a slave, but a son; and since you are a son, God has made you also an heir. *(Galatians 4:7)*

Suggested further reading

Ephesians 2:1–7

Reflect and respond

Do you recognise something in your history that contributed to your low self-esteem?

Have you asked a close friend or minister to pray through some of the issues with you?

Ask God to infuse you with the revelation of your status in Christ.

When You Need Help Making the
Right Choice

*U*nless we have a clear idea of what our priorities should be, we will always be left wondering, "Did I make the right choice?"

I believe that God has an order of priorities for us. If we go by His order we will please Him, we have His authority and things will go well for us. I believe the order is God, our spouse, our children, parents and family, church, good works, personal interests. Some of these categories may not apply to you, you can leave them out. You may want to add others of your own like friends.

Priority does not mean necessarily more time spent. We may spend more time at work, but this does not mean it has top priority. God demands first place – your relationship with Him is what is most important. What you do for others comes out of that. When conflicting demands come it is wonderful to be able to fall back on this order of priorities to guide us, knowing that it has God's authority. Although it is sometimes difficult to be brave enough to follow the order, the price is worth paying.

It is important, too, that even when different demands are not being made on us, we keep to God's order. This is how He has made us, and our lives to function. If we do not, then there can be long-term consequences.

> *"I have so much to do that I spend several hours in prayer before I am able to do it."*
>
> John Wesley

Bible Verses to Help You

"Those who honour me I will honour ..."' *(1 Samuel 2:30)*

"But as for me and my household, we will serve the Lord." *(Joshua 24:15)*

Suggested further reading

Ephesians 3:1–10

Reflect and respond

Have you worked out with God's help what God's priorities are in your life? (What would you least like to lose?)

Do you need to re-order your life to bring it into line with God's order?

When You Experience
Wrong Thoughts

What we hear, or read or watch can change our body chemistry and functioning and affect our feelings. If you watch an exciting film or sporting event on TV, the adrenaline can surge, your pulse race and you feel tense. Reading a newspaper account of a despicable murder, child abuse, or neglect, can make your blood boil, your blood pressure can go up and you feel that you might burst a blood vessel. Listening to a story of heroism or bravery, a child being saved, you can feel a lump in your throat.

Every day the TV brings right into our living rooms news of hate and terrorism and war from the Middle East, Africa, Europe. There are sickening reports on TV and in our newspapers of murder, rape, abuse, violence, burglary.

Perhaps there is little wonder that fed a diet of such things and given what we know about how they affect us, that we can experience thinking out of line with God's best.

While TV can be educational and we should be aware of our world and how we can be salt and light, we should be aware of the effect our reading and viewing has on us.

We should take time to read God's Word (just for ourselves), listen to good music, and uplifting stories. In short, we should take St Paul's advice seriously about what we should be filling our minds with.

"The inward area is the first place of loss of true Christian life, of true spirituality, and the outward sinful act is the result."

Francis Schaeffer

Bible Verses to Help You

Whatever is true ... noble ... right ... pure ... lovely ... admirable – if anything is excellent or praiseworthy – think about such things. *(Philippians 4:8)*

For as [a man] thinks within himself, so he is. *(Proverbs 23:7 NIV footnote)*

Suggested further reading

Romans 12:2

Reflect and respond

Is your daily reading and viewing uplifting?

Do you need to change the balance – choose to fill your mind with that which is holy.

Do you lend an ear to gossip?

When You Need
Cheering Up

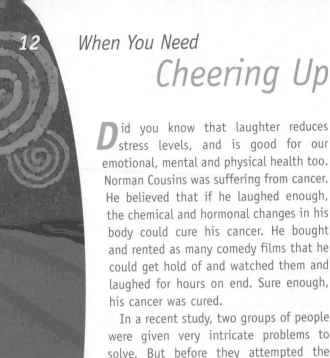

Did you know that laughter reduces stress levels, and is good for our emotional, mental and physical health too. Norman Cousins was suffering from cancer. He believed that if he laughed enough, the chemical and hormonal changes in his body could cure his cancer. He bought and rented as many comedy films that he could get hold of and watched them and laughed for hours on end. Sure enough, his cancer was cured.

In a recent study, two groups of people were given very intricate problems to solve. But before they attempted the problems, one group was asked to watch a quite harrowing documentary video, while the other watched a comedy film. The group who had watched the comedy performed much better at the problem solving than the group who had watched the documentary.

God Himself is the primary source of our joy, and we will experience this as a fruit of the

Spirit (Galatians 5:22), and 1 Thessalonians 1:6 states, "... in spite of severe suffering, you welcomed the message with the joy given by the Holy Spirit". The Bible reveals that we can receive joy directly from God Himself. "May the God of hope fill you with all joy and peace as you trust in him, so that you may overflow with hope by the power of the Holy Spirit" (Romans 15:13). The Father loves to see His children full of joy.

So go on, have a good laugh!

"I guess a man is about as cheerful as he decides to be."

Abraham Lincoln

Bible Verses to Help You

A cheerful heart is good medicine ... *(Proverbs 17:22)*

Our mouths were filled with laughter, our tongues with songs of joy. Then it was said among the nations, "The Lord has done great things for them." *(Psalm 126:2)*

Suggested further reading

Galatians 5:22

Reflect and respond

Where are you seeking to find your joy?

A cheerful look brings joy to the heart (Proverbs 15:30). Do you need to lighten up a bit – should you be smiling more?

Be filled with the Spirit. (Ephesians 5:18)

When Your Security is
Shaken

*T*he stressor that affects more people than any other, and causes most stress, is insecurity or uncertainty. When you feel secure you can relax, and get on with your life. But if you feel insecure, you can become anxious, worried, fearful and stressed about the future. You will probably find it difficult to make decisions.

Many people depend on their position or ministry for security, and if things go awry, security goes and anxiety and stress follow. Recently a large group of male and female civil servants who were in a department threatened with privatisation were compared with another group in a department where no threat existed. There was a marked deterioration in the health of the group under threat compared with the secure group.

You may depend on other things – your career – then you hear that the needs in your chosen field are changing and you wonder if you will be qualified to get a decent job.

Perhaps you have been depending on other people for encouragement and support; but people can let you down.

Are you stressed because your security has been taken away, or is being threatened, or may be in the future? God is the answer, as He is to everything. He is the only person who is entirely dependable and has made us to find our security only in Him. If you put your trust in Him, you are guaranteed absolute security.

> *"I have held many things in my hands, and I have lost them all; but whatever I have placed in God's hands, that I still possess."*
>
> *Martin Luther.*

Bible Verses to Help You

My people have committed two sins: They have forsaken me, the spring of living water, and have dug their own cisterns, broken cisterns that cannot hold water. *(Jeremiah 2:13)*

Some trust in chariots and some in horses, but we trust in the name of the Lord our God. *(Psalm 20:7)*

Suggested further reading

Deuteronomy 33:26–29

Reflect and respond

Do you feel insecure, fearful of the future – what are you depending on for your security?

Are these sources utterly dependable?

Only God is fully dependable. Are you building your life on the Rock?

14

When Counting the Cost of
Discipleship

Jesus speaks a number of times about the cost of following Him. In Luke 14:27 He says, "Anyone who does not carry his cross and follow me cannot be my disciple". We may find it hard to understand what taking up our cross is all about.

The principle of Jesus taking up His cross was not the burden of it, but the willingness. He laid aside everything else, facing His only objective, that of doing His Father's will. He could say to His Father, "not my will, but yours be done".

Discipleship is always based on an attitude of heart and mind, and the willingness and obedience which follows. We need to consider our position with Jesus, and the depth of commitment we are prepared to make. The more we know and appreciate God's redeeming work in our lives, the simpler taking up our cross can become.

Paul took up his cross from the moment of his amazing encounter with Jesus. He let go of everything both past and personal, in order that he might know God in the deepest relationship possible. His conversion was so life-changing, that knowing God became his consuming passion, it outweighed every other desire in his life, he considered "everything a loss compared to the surpassing greatness of knowing Christ Jesus my Lord" (Philippians 3:8). He counted the cost and decided to stake everything on being a true disciple.

"It seems amazingly difficult to put on the yoke of Christ, but immediately we do put it on, everything becomes easy."

Oswald Chambers

Bible Verses to Help You

What is more, I consider everything a loss compared to the surpassing greatness of knowing Christ Jesus my Lord, for whose sake I have lost all things. I consider them rubbish, that I may gain Christ and be found in him, not having a righteousness of my own that comes from the law, but that which is through faith in Christ – the righteousness that comes from God and is by faith. *(Philippians 3:8–9)*

And if anyone gives even a cup of cold water to one of these little ones because he is my disciple, I tell you the truth, he will certainly not lose his reward." *(Matthew 10:42)*

Suggested further reading

Psalm 130:1–8

Reflect and respond

Ask yourself how much are you prepared to count the cost of following Jesus.

15

When Life is a
Battle

*I*n one sense, life is always a battle and if God has his place as Lord in our life, then Satan has a vested interest in breaking down that stronghold. But, remember, *we are on the winning side*. God has already defeated Satan on the cross, and has provided all the resources for us to keep him at bay in our lives.

Prayer is a key area here, and sometimes the hardest thing of all, maybe because it requires the greatest measure of discipline. The majority of Christians struggle in this area. Yet this is the greatest gift available to us, all day and every day, the opportunity of communication with God, the connection from earth to heaven. Without communication, we are either living in unreality or history, but with prayer at our disposal we can know the living ongoing reality of walking with God. There are different kinds of prayer, and varying depths of prayer. We can talk to God anywhere and anytime, but to allow ourselves to hear and receive from God involves giving our time, and shutting out everything else. This can be costly, but can also reap great rewards. This is where the battles are won and the victories claimed. Let us make this our starting point.

"One with God is a majority."

Billy Graham

Bible Verses to Help You

The earnest, (heartfelt, continued) prayer of a righteous man makes tremendous power available – dynamic in its working. *(James 5:16 Amplified Version).*

"Finally, be strong in the Lord and his mighty power." *(Ephesians 6:10)*

Suggested further reading

Ephesians 1:11–23

Reflect and respond

Prayer changes things.

The victory is ours for the claiming.

Declare your victory in the light of your inheritance.

16

When the Burden Gets Too *Heavy*

Do you ever feel overburdened? Most people do at some time or other. It is not unusual, but it is important how we handle the situation.

In the teachings of Jesus we read on several occasions of His comparison to the burden carried by oxen ploughing the fields. He tells us that if we are yoked together in harmony with Him, we will find that His yoke is the kind that fits perfectly, and working in unison with Him we will find that our task or burden is light.

In Bible times strong men who earned their living by carrying heavy goods could be seen slowly plodding along the road under huge loads of luggage, or furniture. Then when they needed to rest they would stop and another man would come alongside and put his shoulder under the burden and take the weight for five or ten minutes.

So our problem is not having burdens, but rather how we handle them. Do you need the help of Jesus so that as you work together in partnership you can experience the joy of a shared lightweight burden? Or are you carrying a burden that you don't need to carry at all? If so, ask Jesus to come alongside so that you can make a transfer.

No burden is too heavy when it is carried with love.

Bible Verses to Help You

"Casting the whole of your care, all your anxieties, all your worries, all your concerns, once and for all, on Him ..."

(1 Peter 5:7 Amplified Version)

... you are with me; your rod and your staff, they comfort me.
(Psalm 23:4b)

Suggested further reading

Psalm 55:1–23

Reflect and respond

Carrying a burden may be a necessity, carrying it alone is optional.

Try and express your feelings to God in prayer.

17

When Trusting is
Hard

Do you worry about tomorrow? Do you inwardly struggle to work out whether there will be enough money for food, clothes and mortgage? And what about resources and help needed in the home?

Jesus teaches us in simple terms to trust Him one day at a time, and He will provide on that basis. We may sometimes feel as though we have suddenly run into a crisis, but God is never taken by surprise, He knows our needs better than we know ourselves, God's provision is, PRO (before) VISION (seeing), and it is very reassuring to know that He sees our needs in advance.

In Luke 12, starting at verse 22, Jesus says, "Do not worry about your life, what you will eat; or about your body, what you will wear. Life is more than food, and the body more than clothes ... Consider how the lilies grow. They do not labour or spin. Yet I tell you, not even Solomon in all his splendour was dressed like one of these. If that is how God clothes the grass of the field, which is here today, and tomorrow is thrown into the fire, how much more will he clothe you, O you of little faith."

Let us take this opportunity to open up ourselves to new areas of trust, and experience a greater dependency on God. By this we can know a greater measure of His faithfulness and provision for our needs.

"Worry is an indication that we think God cannot look after us."
Oswald Chambers

Bible Verses to Help You
"So do not worry, saying, 'What shall we eat?' or 'What shall we drink?' or 'What shall we wear?' For the pagans run after all these things, and your heavenly Father knows that you need them. But seek first his kingdom and his righteousness, and all these things will be given to you as well. Therefore do not worry about tomorrow, for tomorrow will worry about itself. Each day has enough trouble of its own."
(Matthew 6:31–34)

Suggested further reading
Psalm 95:1–7

Reflect and respond
Meditate on how faithful God has been in your life to date and praise Him for it.

Not to worry is a command not an option. Decide, with God's help, not to worry but trust.

18

When Caught in
Debt

*S*adly, when the unexpected happens financially, very few of us know what to do next. The main reason for this is that we have never been taught about handling money. Most people tend to live up to, or usually just beyond their means, and use credit to enable them to do so. Remarkably, the more we earn the more we borrow. Is it any wonder then that panic sets in when we hit a major reverse?

It is a lack of financial education that often leads us into crisis in the first place. We happily take on commitments, which if we had budgeted we would have known we could not afford. We tend to spend addictively and impulsively, and often significantly underestimate our necessary outgoings. When an unexpected adverse event, such as an interest rise or major car repair occurs, we have no resources to cover it. We also tend to believe what we are told and what we are sold. Many of us don't bother with the small print because we haven't understood the large.

But not only do we need sound practical teaching we also need sound biblical teaching. The Bible says more about handling money and possessions than most other subjects. The world about us shouts "spend, spend, spend", but Jesus quietly asks us to wait and listen and learn from Him. We need to set our eyes on things above and learn to be good stewards of God's resources.

"There is nothing wrong with people possessing riches. The wrong comes when riches possess people."

Billy Graham

Bible Verses to Help You

And my God shall supply all your need according to His riches in glory by Christ Jesus. Now to our God and Father be glory forever and ever. Amen. *(Philippians 4:19–20)*

"Do not store up for yourselves treasures on earth, where moth and rust destroy, and where thieves break in and steal. But store up for yourselves treasures in heaven … For where your treasure is, there your heart will be also. *(Matthew 6:19–21)*

Suggested further reading

Proverbs 16:19–23

Reflect and respond

Set your mind that, with God's help, you will straighten out your finances.

Don't be ashamed to seek expert help.

19

When You need to Re-establish a
Relationship

Relationships are sometimes the most difficult but always the most important things to maintain (particularly a marriage relationship). And the onus is always on me! Someone has said, "If my brother draws a circle to exclude me, I must draw a bigger circle to include him."

Among the first actions you will need to take to re-establish a relationship will be to recognise the need to say sorry and to ask forgiveness for past hurts which you may have inflicted. All the old rubbish that has been put in the waste bin has to be taken out and dealt with. Learn to communicate – no matter how big or small things have been, or how silly they may seem. Work them through together to resolve them. Doing this brings you closer to each other and pushes the enemy out. Dismiss all thoughts of selfishness, you are in this together.

By giving love away you will receive it back in full measure, pressed down and overflowing

(Luke 6:38). The Bible says "Cast your bread upon the waters" (Ecclesiastes 11:1), and if you cast your love upon the one with whom relationship has broken down, it will come back to you. Loving someone else is wanting the very best for them, as God wants the very best for you.

It will take time to rebuild and building is a gradual process. Learn to stand upon the Rock and trust, not only each other, but also God in all of this. Know that your Father has your highest interests at heart. The benefits far outweigh the cost.

"Reconciliation is not weakness or cowardice. It demands courage, nobility, generosity, sometimes heroism, an overcoming of oneself rather than of one's adversary."

Pope Paul VI

Bible Verses to Help You

"A new command I give you: Love one another. As I have loved you, so you must love one another." *(John 13:34)*

"Therefore, if you are offering your gift at the altar and there remember that your brother has something against you, leave your gift there in front of the altar. First go and be reconciled to your brother; then come and offer your gift." *(Matthew 5:23–24)*

Suggested further reading

Genesis 45

Reflect and respond

Remember – Jesus said, "Blessed are the peacemakers". If you want to be blessed, be a peacemaker.

20

When God Seems
Far Away

Sometimes even mature Christians who have followed the Lord for many years go through times when God seems very far away. In the main there are three possible reasons for this.

First, the problem can stem from a purely physical cause. Sickness, stress or overwork can affect our moods to such a degree that we think we are spiritually low when the real problem lies in a poor physical condition. This is why God gave Elijah a period of rest and recuperation (see 1 Kings 19).

Second, God might seem far away because of sin. God has so built our spiritual system that when we sin, conviction descends. In this situation repentance is the only way back. Repentance, remember, means more than just "being sorry"; it means being sorry enough to quit. When repentance has taken effect we can be sure that our relationship with God will be restored.

The third reason – and by far the most common one – for feeling that God is far away is because we fail to take the time to maintain our relationship with Him. If we don't take the time to talk to God regularly in prayer and listen to Him through reading His Word, then ought it to surprise us that the relationship between us and Him begins to deteriorate? As someone put it: "if God seems far away – guess who moved?" God never moves away from us – it's we who move away from Him.

"Thou hast made us for Thyself, O Lord; and our heart is restless until it rests in Thee."

St Augustine

Bible Verses to Help You

God has said, "Never will I leave you; never will I forsake you." *(Hebrews 13:5b)*

"God did this so that men would seek him and perhaps reach out for him and find him, though he is not far from each one of us. 'For in him we live and move and have our being'." *(Acts 17:27–28)*

Suggested further reading

Psalm 139:7–10

Reflect and respond

Do you need a physical health check-up?

Have you dealt with any unresolved sin?

Have you spent quality time with God lately?

21

When Fear
Transcends

*F*ear, it must be said at once, can be a friend as well as a foe. A healthy fear keeps us from rushing across a traffic-infested street, it compels caution and preserves life. An unhealthy fear, however, can quickly enslave the whole personality.

How does Christ enable His children to deal with fear? He does it by imparting to us the energy and power to face anything that comes, assuring us that whatever the difficulties we have to face, we can be more than a match for them, in Him. The apostle Paul puts it like this: "For God did not give us a spirit of timidity, but a spirit of power, of love and of self-discipline" (2 Timothy 1:7).

The one thing that underlies all unhealthy fear is the desire for avoidance. The fearful heart says: "When afraid – avoid." The Holy Spirit, however, enables us to face whatever it is that troubles us, knowing that no matter what happens it can never separate us from God and His unending love. The apostle John says, "Perfect love drives out fear" (1 John 4:18). Resting in His love – a love that will never let us go – we can move into any situation that makes us afraid with a confidence that transcends all fear. Fear says: "Avoid." Faith says, "Confront." Therefore move with God towards the thing you fear and just see what God will do.

"Faith is not a sword just to grab ... faith is a way of life. Feed your faith and starve your doubts to death!"

Lester Sumrall

Bible Verses to Help You

Even though I walk through the valley of the shadow of death, I will fear no evil, for you are with me; your rod and your staff, they comfort me. *(Psalm 23:4)*

The Lord is my light and my salvation – whom shall I fear? *(Psalm 27:1)*

Suggested further reading.

Psalm 46:1–2

Reflect and respond

Is your fear a godly or worldly fear?

Have you strengthened your spirit with the Word?

Have you been avoiding rather than confronting your fear?

22

When It's Difficult to be
Generous

Perhaps nothing is as revealing of our dedication to Christ and His cause as our attitude towards money. Jesus, in the Gospels, talked a great deal about money. And why? Because the itch for money is in most palms, and He knew that unless His followers have thought clearly about their attitude towards money, they can never become mature disciples.

When we consider material possessions we face a sharp issue, for either we will transform the material into the image of the spiritual or the material will transform us into its own image. Material things must be surrendered to God – if not we will soon find ourselves surrendering to the material. Some Christians give a tenth of their income to God, and for those on low incomes that is a fine thing. Others with higher incomes, however, find they can give away more than a tithe without incurring any hardship. A businessman put it wisely when he said: "Everything I own is

God's and my constant prayer is this: 'Lord, how much of Your money can I keep for myself?' " That is the right priority, for everything we needlessly spend on ourselves prevents us from ministering to the needs of others. Holding our possessions at God's disposal means our trust is in Him, not in money.

We must allow God to open up our clenched fists and be as generous to others as He is to us. All giving ought to be in gratitude for what He has given to us.

"Money has never yet made anyone rich."
Lucius Annaeus Seneca

Bible Verses to Help You

A generous man will prosper; he who refreshes others will himself be refreshed. *(Proverbs 11:25)*

"Give, and it will be given to you. A good measure, pressed down, shaken together and running over, will be poured into your lap. For with the measure you use, it will be measured to you." *(Luke 6:38)*

Suggested further reading

2 Corinthians 9:6–8

Reflect and respond

Have you surrendered your possessions to God?

Do you recognise and live by God's principles as far as money, giving and receiving are concerned?

23

When Forgiving is Not *Easy*

*S*ome think Christianity sets an impossible standard when it calls on believers to forgive all those who have hurt or injured them. But with God "all things are possible". There are three main reasons why we may find it difficult to forgive.

First, we do not have a sufficiently deep realisation of how much we ourselves have been forgiven. The sin of another against us is as nothing when compared to our sin against God – yet He has forgiven us.

Second, holding resentment or indignation against another who has hurt us gives us a sense of power and control over them, and when we give it up, we are left feeling somewhat helpless. But it is to helplessness we are called in the words: "'It is mine to avenge, I will repay,' says the Lord" (Romans 12:19). Forgiveness involves giving up control and trusting God with the outcome.

A third reason is what we might call "misplaced dependency". This occurs when we move from dependency on God to dependency on others. Then when they hurt us, we stumble because we believe we need them in order to function. This is why we are always hurt most by those who are closest to us.

Forgiveness, we must remember, is not so much a feeling but a decision – an action of the will. You decide to forgive, whether you feel like it or not. *You supply the willingness, God will supply the power.*

"The greatest single cause of atheism ... is Christians who acknowledge Jesus with their lips ... and deny Him by their lifestyle. ..."

Brennan Manning

Bible Verses to Help You

Bear with each other and forgive whatever grievances you may have against one another. Forgive as the Lord forgave you. *(Colossians 3:13)*

... as far as the east is from the west, so far has he removed our transgressions from us. *(Psalm 103:12)*

Suggested further reading

2 Corinthians 2:8–11

Reflect and respond

Do you feel overwhelmed with your unforgiveness? Go to the Father with your problem.

Have you made the decision to forgive?

24

When You No Longer Want to
Pray

*T*he obstacles to prayer are many. Some claim they don't have time to pray, others that they have no place to pray. Well, it's always possible to go for a walk with Jesus. Still others complain they don't know what to pray for. Then make a list – friends and loved ones who need to be converted, those known to you who are sick, the needs of the church you attend, your own needs, and so on.

By far the most common obstacle to prayer, however, is disinclination. People do not pray because they do not feel like it. But we must not assume that prayer is effective only when it arises from an eager and emotional heart. Those who have achieved great power in prayer tell us that floods of feeling come only now and again in their times of intercession. If we have an appointment to meet someone whom we regard as important, do we break it a few moments before the meeting because we feel disinclined? Common courtesy tells us it would not be right. Are we to be less courteous with God?

The great practitioners of prayer assure us God can do more with us when we pray against our inclination than when we pray with it. The willingness to submit to Him deepens our surrender; our resolve to go to God builds steel into our Christian commitment. It is faith, not feeling, that measures the efficacy of prayer.

> *"Intercessory prayer might be defined as loving our neighbour on our knees."*
>
> Charles Brent

25

When Doubts
Crowd In

Many Christians feel that if doubt exists in their minds they cannot be true believers. This arises from a wrong understanding of the nature of doubt. "Doubt," says Os Guinness, "is a state of mind in suspension between faith and unbelief so that it is neither of them wholly, and it is each only partly. It is faith in two minds."

Perhaps we can better understand doubt by taking the analogy of fear. Many think fear is the opposite of courage, but it is not. The opposite of fear is cowardice. Fear is the half-way stage between the two. It is not wrong to feel fear in certain situations. The real question is what do we do with it – something courageous or something cowardly? It is the same with doubt. It stands undecided between faith and unbelief and has to choose between the two.

A man one day came to Jesus and confessed to his struggle with doubt (Mark 9:14–29). The struggle with doubt must be seen as a sign of faith, not unbelief.

What destroys faith is not doubt but disobedience – the unwillingness to bring those doubts and lay them at the feet of Jesus. The prayer of the man in the incident referred to, "I do believe; help me overcome my unbelief!" is one that all of us must echo whenever we are caught in the throes of doubt. This attitude changes everything.

> "Believe your beliefs and doubt your doubts."
>
> F.F. Bosworth

Bible Verses to Help You

Then he said to Thomas, "Put your finger here; see my hands. Reach out your hand and put it into my side. Stop doubting and believe." Thomas said to him, "My Lord and my God!"
(John 20:27–28)

Immediately Jesus reached out his hand and caught him. "You of little faith," he said, "why did you doubt?"
(Matthew 14:31)

Suggested further reading

Job 42:1–5

Reflect and respond

Stop mentally beating yourself up when you doubt.

Do you wallow in doubt, or use it as a springboard to faith?

Call upon God to deliver you from doubt.

26

When Dealing with
Failure

*I*t's hard to look objectively at things when one has failed. When Millais first exhibited his "Ophelia" in 1852 one critic dubbed it "O Failure!" It is said that Millais was plagued by these words for the rest of his life.

When overtaken by failure sit down as soon as possible and prayerfully begin to analyse the reason for the failure. Consider the possibility that God may have allowed this failure because it was part of His purpose for your life. Many have discovered that God allowed failure in their life to turn their thoughts in a new direction of service for Him.

If, however, after prayer and careful consideration of this possibility you are sure you have God's approval for continuing along the same lines, then ask yourself, Have I contributed to this failure by wrong timing, failure to weigh up the pros and cons, disregard of moral principles, insensitivity to other people's feelings ... and so on? Having learned the lessons that come from failure – try again.

A Christian poster I once saw showed a man in a T-shirt with the admission "I gave up". In the corner of the poster, barely visible, was a drawing of a little black hill and on it a very tiny cross. These words were printed beneath it: "I didn't." The One who triumphed over all obstacles holds out His hands to you. Take His hand and if another purpose has not been shown you – try again.

> *"The worst is not to fail, but to give up."*
>
> *Ed Cole*

Bible Verses to Help You

If the Lord delights in a man's way, he makes his steps firm; though he stumble, he will not fall, for the Lord upholds him with his hand. *(Psalm 37:23–24)*

I press on towards the goal to win the prize for which God has called me heavenwards in Christ Jesus. *(Philippians 3:14)*

Suggested further reading

Proverbs 3:1–5

Reflect and respond

Are your goals God's goals?

Have you taken responsibility for your own actions?

Trust God to deliver you in your circumstances.

27

When Hopes are *Dashed*

*H*ope is one of the cardinal values of the Christian faith. "And now these three remain," said the apostle Paul in 1 Corinthians 13:13, "faith, hope and love." All through the New Testament, hope is spoken of in the highest terms.

We must differentiate, however, between the word "hope" as it is used in Scripture and the way it is used in ordinary conversation. Sometimes people say, "I hope things will get better," or "I am hoping for an increase in my salary," but we are not given any guarantees in Scripture that everything we "hope" for in this sense will come our way. When the Bible talks about "hope" it is talking about the certainty we have as Christians that God's eternal purposes will never be thwarted. The thing that gives a Christian what the writer to the Hebrews calls a hope "both sure and steadfast" (Hebrews 6:19, AV) is the fact that God is on the throne. Have you noticed in the Scriptures that whenever

God's servants were in trouble they were given a vision of the eternal throne? Isaiah ... David ... Ezekiel ... the apostle John. Why a throne? Because God rules from His throne, and no matter if appearances are to the contrary, He is always in control. The hope (or certainty) that God's purposes continue even if ours get pushed aside acts as an anchor to the soul. We must never forget it.

"Fulfilment of your destiny does not come in a moment, a month, or a year, but over a lifetime."

Casey Treat

Bible Verses to Help You

We have this hope as an anchor for the soul, firm and secure. It enters the inner sanctuary behind the curtain ...
(Hebrews 6:19)

Know therefore that the Lord your God is God; he is the faithful God, keeping his covenant of love to a thousand generations of those who love him and keep his commands.
(Deuteronomy 7:9)

Suggested further reading
Hebrews 11

Reflect and respond
Is your hope in God or mere speculation?
Have you allowed His Word to fuel your hope?
Trust the Father, and watch your hope soar.

28

When You Fall into *Grievous Sin*

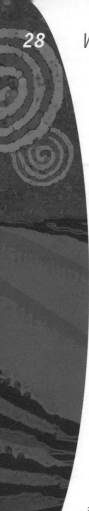

Sin, it has been said, is not so much the breaking of God's laws as the breaking of His heart. How then do we relieve the hurt that lies upon the heart of God when we have fallen into grievous sin?

First, we must not minimise the sin. Nowadays there is a tendency to describe a moral mishap as just a "little" thing, or "it wasn't important". Cancer in the stomach is still cancer even though a person may pass off their discomfort as "a bit of indigestion". We don't make a deadly thing innocuous by giving it a different name.

Second, we must confess the sin to God. We must cry out to Him as did the psalmist, "Have mercy on me, O God, according to your unfailing love ... blot out my transgressions. Wash away all my iniquity and cleanse me from my sin" (Psalm 51:1–2).

Third, if the sin has involved others then we must seek to put things right with them also. It is always helpful to discuss this matter with a minister or a Christian counsellor, however, before embarking on a course of action so as to avoid unnecessary complications.

Fourth, we must walk into the future clean and more dependent than ever on God's empowering grace. All the resources of heaven are engaged against sin, and the reason why we fall into it is because we do not avail ourselves of those resources.

> *"Get alone with Jesus – and either tell Him that you do not want sin to die out in you – or else tell Him that at all costs you want to be identified with His death."*
>
> *Oswald Chambers*

Bible Verses to Help You

If we confess our sins, he is faithful and just and will forgive us our sins and purify us from all unrighteousness.
(1 John 1:9)

Blessed is he whose transgressions are forgiven, whose sins are covered. Blessed is the man whose sin the Lord does not count against him and in whose spirit is no deceit.
(Psalm 32:1–2)

Suggested further reading

James 4:6–10

Reflect and respond

Have you taken responsibility for your sin?

Have you confessed your sin and settled things with others?

Look to your future with a clean heart and lean upon His grace.

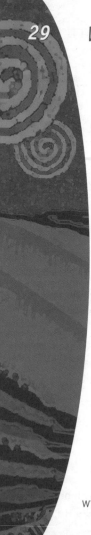

29

When Scripture Fails to Come *Alive*

*T*he Bible is the most fascinating, engrossing and sustaining Book in the world. Hebrews 4:12 describes it like this: "For the word of God is living and active. Sharper than any double-edged sword, it penetrates even to dividing soul and spirit, joints and marrow; it judges the thoughts and attitudes of the heart." Why then should the Bible sometimes fail to impact our lives?

There are several reasons for this – reading it too hurriedly, coming to it from a sense of duty rather than expectantly, being preoccupied with other things. But the major reason why the Bible does not impact our lives is our unwillingness to let it search our hearts. *We will never really get much out of the Bible until we come to it with exposure in mind.* In other words, *we must not be content with just reading the Bible, we must let the Bible read us.*

When we approach the Bible in this way we will discover it is more shocking than supportive, more convicting than comforting. That is not to say it does not comfort us when in distress, for it most certainly does. Its *main* function, though, is to expose our wrong assumptions about life and to replace them with biblical perspectives. When we approach the Scriptures with the attitude of heart that says, "Speak Lord, thy servant heareth," the promise of Hebrews 4:12 cannot fail to come true.

> *"A new world will arise out of the religious mists when we approach our Bible with the idea that it is ... a book which is now speaking."*
>
> A.W. Tozer

Bible Verses to Help You

Search me, O God, and know my heart; test me and know my anxious thoughts. See if there is any offensive way in me, and lead me in the way everlasting. *(Psalm 139:23–24)*

Let me understand the teaching of your precepts; then I will meditate on your wonders. *(Psalm 119:27)*

Suggested further reading

Deuteronomy 8:1–5

Reflect and respond

Reflect on your approach to reading the Bible – do you let the Bible read you?

Have you set aside a time and a place to let God speak to you every day through His Word?

30

When Coping with
Depression

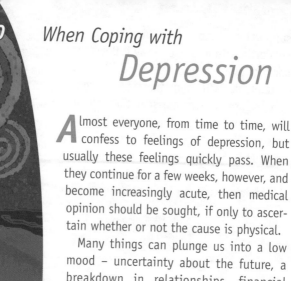

*A*lmost everyone, from time to time, will confess to feelings of depression, but usually these feelings quickly pass. When they continue for a few weeks, however, and become increasingly acute, then medical opinion should be sought, if only to ascertain whether or not the cause is physical.

Many things can plunge us into a low mood – uncertainty about the future, a breakdown in relationships, financial difficulties, ageing, lack of purpose, and so on. The common denominator, though, with deeply depressed feelings is a sense of loss. A vital clue also to understanding what plunges us into depression is found when we examine the relationship between what we are doing and the expected rewards. If our actions and behaviours do not, over a period of time, bring us the rewards we expect then we can become so discouraged that we sink into a low mood.

The best remedy for all non-biological

depression is to gain a new perspective – to turn one's gaze from earth to heaven. The psalmist in Psalm 42 sees that there is a thirst inside him that no one can meet except God. When he looks to God for the satisfaction of that thirst (rather than others), his soul then rests on the hope that no matter what happens, he remains secure as a person. Understanding this, and constantly applying it in our lives, is the key to overcoming and remaining free from depression.

"Though I sit in darkness, the Lord will be my light."

Micah 7:8

Bible Verses to Help You

Why are you downcast, O my soul? Why so disturbed within me? Put your hope in God, for I will yet praise him, my Saviour and my God. *(Psalm 42:5)*

The Lord is close to the broken-hearted and saves those who are crushed in spirit. *(Psalm 34:18)*

Suggested further reading

Psalm 32:1–7

Reflect and respond,

Is your depression medically related?

Is your gaze towards heaven or earth?

Thirst after God and regain your hope.

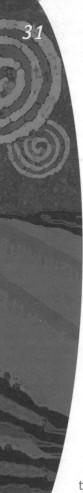

31

When You Doubt that God is
Good

"*T*he root of sin", said Oswald Chambers, "is the belief that God is not good." There are a multitude of circumstances and events we have to face in a fallen world that suggest God is not good – earthquakes, famines, storms and floods that wipe out whole communities, disease, and so on.

Before radar was invented, the art of navigation depended on the existence of fixed points. Mariners took their bearings not from a cloud or a floating spar but from the stars and from things that were solid, such as a headland or a lighthouse. If a seaman took a bearing and found he was off course he would not doubt the star or the headland – he would doubt himself.

We need to do the same whenever we find ourselves doubting that God is good. We must see to it that we are fixed to the things that are fixed. The cross is one of those things. It is the irrefutable proof that God is love. When we look around and consider the many situations that seem to give the lie to the fact that God is love, we must not pretend these matters do not cause us problems. Rather, we must set them all over against the one thing that is crystal clear – God's love as demonstrated for us on Calvary. A God who would do that for us simply must be Love. *At the foot of Calvary the ground is fixed.*

"In the maddening maze of things, And tossed by storm and flood, To one fixed trust my spirit clings: I know that God is good!"
John Greenleaf Whittier.

Bible Verses to Help You

"Why do you call me good?" Jesus answered. "No-one is good – except God alone." *(Mark 10:18)*

For God so loved the world that he gave his one and only Son, that whoever believes in him shall not perish but have eternal life. For God did not send his Son into the world to condemn the world, but to save the world through him. *(John 3:16–17)*

Suggested further reading

1 Peter 2:1–5

Reflect and respond

Is your thinking grounded in the Scriptures?

Have you confused worldly circumstances with God's will?

Fix your eyes once again on Calvary and God's love displayed there.

32

When Facing Bitter
Disappointment

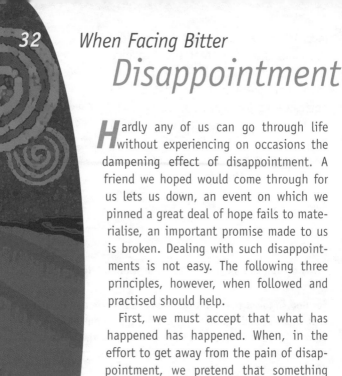

*H*ardly any of us can go through life without experiencing on occasions the dampening effect of disappointment. A friend we hoped would come through for us lets us down, an event on which we pinned a great deal of hope fails to materialise, an important promise made to us is broken. Dealing with such disappointments is not easy. The following three principles, however, when followed and practised should help.

First, we must accept that what has happened has happened. When, in the effort to get away from the pain of disappointment, we pretend that something has not happened, or that it has happened in a different way, we deceive ourselves. Integrity requires that whatever is true, whatever is real, must be faced.

Second, we must acknowledge our feelings. If we feel hurt, angry, frustrated, or any other negative emotions, we must be willing to face them. Unacknowledged emotions invariably cause trouble.

Third, we must bring the issue to God in prayer, remembering that He can take every one of life's disappointments and make them work for us rather than against us (see Romans 8:28–29). Just change the first letter of "Disappointment" from "D" to "H" and "*Disappointment*" becomes "*His-appointment*".

> "Deep in
> unfathamable
> mines of never
> failing skill,
> He treasures up
> His bright
> designs,
> And works His
> sovereign will."
>
> William Cowper

Bible Verses to Help You

And we know that in all things God works for the good of those who love him, who have been called according to his purpose. *(Romans 8:28)*

Trust in the Lord with all your heart and lean not on your own understanding; in all your ways acknowledge him, and he will make your paths straight. *(Proverbs 3:5–6)*

Suggested further reading

Proverbs 16:1–9

Reflect and respond

Accept what has happened, or not happened, and bring your feelings to God knowing that He never disappoints.

33

When You Need Divine
Guidance

*F*ew Christians have difficulty believing in the personal guidance of God. For the most part our difficulty is not with the fact that God guides but how. Usually God guides along five main routes: through prayerful reading of the Scriptures, through the preaching of God's Word, through reason, through circumstances, and through a strong inner witness. How do these all come together when we are in need of personal guidance?

Some people have found God's guidance while prayerfully reading His Word, as a certain verse is quickened to them. Others have heard His voice through a sermon in church. Still others find the divine will by reasoning an issue through, either by themselves or with a godly friend or counsellor. Circumstances can point the way to God's will also. Things may get chaotic, but often God shakes our circumstances to move us in a different direction.

Then finally there is what some Christians

call the way of peace. To find guidance it can help to look at the various options open to you, then picture yourself going down them one by one. On one of these paths a deeper peace may rest. Not a thrill, not pleasure, but peace. This may be the road down which God wants you to travel. Remember, however, it's always good to share all your conclusions about God's guidance, if you can, with a wise and godly friend.

"Abraham did not know the way, but he knew the Guide."

Lee Robertson

Trust in the Lord with all your heart and lean not on your own understanding; in all your ways acknowledge him, and he will make your paths straight. *(Proverbs 3:5–6)*

Your word is a lamp to my feet and a light for my path. *(Psalm 119:105)*

Suggested further reading
Psalm 25:1–5

Reflect and respond

What have you done so far to seek God for guidance?

Have you sought Him in His Word and with prayer?

Have you established an "inner witness" that brings peace to your chosen path?

34

When You Feel Forgotten by *God*

*I*t is forgivable, when overtaken by all kinds of difficulties and problems, to think that we are forgotten by God. Forgivable, but not true. From observation and experience it appears that the Christians who fall prey to this misapprehension are those who struggle with a deep sense of inferiority and see themselves as being of little consequence on this earth. Feeling of little importance on earth they deduce, erroneously, they are of little importance in heaven. The psalmist reminds us in Psalm 139 that God's thoughts are always towards us and that they are more in number than the grains of sand (v.18).

But perhaps the greatest verse we can focus our attention on when tempted to think that God has forgotten us is Isaiah 49:16: "See, I have engraved you on the palms of my hands." The palm of the hand has passed into our proverbs as a symbol of familiarity. We sometimes hear people say: "I know it like the palm of my hand." It is on the palm of His hand, says the prophet Isaiah, that God has put our names. And they are not just written there, but engraved there. This means our names are before Him in such a way that they cannot be overlooked. He does not depend on a ministering spirit to bring our names to His attention. They are imprinted there – on the palms of His hands.

"God's investment in us is so great he could not possibly abandon us."

Erwin W. Lutzer.

Bible Verses to Help You

"Can a mother forget the baby at her breast and have no compassion on the child she has borne? Though she may forget, I will not forget you!" *(Isaiah 49:15)*

Suggested further reading

Exodus 34:1–7

Reflect and respond

Have you swallowed the lie of the enemy that God does not care?

Have you sought the security of the Scriptures to see the true Father?

Bask in the knowledge that God knows you personally.

35

When Battling with Sexual
Frustration

*T*he hunger for sex, we must recognise, is no more shameful than the hunger for food. However, this should not be taken to mean that, like the hunger for food, it must be indulged. We can't live without food, but we can live without sex.

The main problem underlying sexual frustration is that of the release of sexual energy. With married people this can be done legitimately through the act of sexual intercourse, but for single people this is forbidden by Scripture. How do single people, and in some circumstances married people also, handle a clamant sex drive? Is masturbation the answer? Scripture is relatively silent on this issue, and some feel that when no other relief can be found, masturbation is permissible, providing no sexual images are being entertained.

There is "a more excellent way", though – the way of sublimation. Sublimation is the rechannelling of energies into another and higher level of activity. One of the best practitioners of this was the apostle Paul. He was creative at the place of the mind and spirit, thus his lower drives were being sublimated.

When all the energies of the spirit are focused on Christ and His kingdom, sexual energies will not be eliminated, but they will be prevented from causing frustration. Many single persons with a strong sex drive have found that it loses its persistent power when they lose themselves in strong service for the Master.

> *"The more a man denies himself, the more shall he obtain from God."*
>
> Horace Bushnell

Bible Verses to Help You

Therefore, I urge you, brothers, in view of God's mercy, to offer your bodies as living sacrifices, holy and pleasing to God – this is your spiritual act of worship. *(Romans 12:1)*

Just as you used to offer the parts of your body in slavery to impurity and to ever-increasing wickedness, so now offer them in slavery to righteousness leading to holiness. *(Romans 6:19)*

Suggested further reading

1 Corinthians 6:18–20

Reflect and respond

Are your motivations dominated by the flesh?

Have you placed sexual desire in proper context?

Place you energies in wholehearted devotion to God and His kingdom.

36

When God's Promises are
Delayed

*T*he Scriptures are full of instances of people struggling to make sense of God's delays. Take, for example, Abraham's long wait for a son. Or Joseph's extended years in prison as a victim of cruel circumstances. When something that God has promised is slow in coming to pass, life can become very confusing and perplexing. We look at opportunities that are being missed and cry out: "Why? Why? Why?"

The first thing we should do when faced by a delayed promise is to check that we received a divine promise in the first place and that we are not victims of wishful thinking. Many take words from the Bible which were meant only for certain people in Scripture, apply them to themselves, and then become disappointed when they do not come to pass. So check to see that it was a clear promise God gave you from His Word.

Once you are sure of this then keep in mind

that God brings things to pass at precisely the right time. There must be no equivocation on this point, for once we question the fact of God's perfect timing we open ourselves up to all kind of doubts. We can't stop doubt entering our heart, of course, but we can stop it lodging there. Whatever God has promised you (and you are sure it is a promise), then rest assured it will come to pass. Not always in your time. But always in His.

"Faith takes God without any ifs. If God says anything, faith says, 'I believe it'; faith says, 'Amen' to it."

D.L. Moody

Bible Verses to Help You

For he remembered his holy promise given to his servant Abraham. *(Psalm 105:42)*

Let us hold unswervingly to the hope we profess, for he who promised is faithful. *(Hebrews 10:23)*

Suggested further reading
Habakkuk 2:1–3

Reflect and respond
Are questions over God's timing dominating your life?
Are your sure of God's promises to you?
Trust that the Father has your life in His faithful hands.

37

When Your Love for the Lord Begins to *Wane*

*I*t should always cause us great concern when our love for the Lord Jesus Christ diminishes and wanes. Our love for Christ, we must always remember, is a response to His love for us. "We love because he first loved us", says the apostle John in 1 John 4:19. Our souls are designed to respond to divine love, not manufacture it. When we focus on how much we are loved by Him, and allow ourselves to be impacted by that fact, it will inevitably create a response in us. However, it must be emphasised that this principle will only work when sin has been put out of our hearts. In Revelation 2:4 our Lord says to the church in Ephesus: "I have this against you, that you have left your first love" (NKJ). Note they had not lost their love, but left it.

There is a great difference between losing something and leaving it. We leave our love for Christ when we violate one or more of His commandments, and love cannot be recovered until sin is confessed and God's forgiveness sought.

Once all is dealt with then the principle mentioned above should be followed – focus not so much on how you can love Him but on His love for you. Gaze on the cross, see love bleeding for you. The greater your awareness of how much you are loved, the greater will be your response.

"I love, my God, but with no love of mine,

For I have none to give;

I love thee, Lord, but all the love is thine,

For by thy love I live."

Jeanne Marie de la Mothe Guyon

Bible Verses to Help You

How great is the love the Father has lavished on us, that we should be called children of God! And that is what we are! *(1 John 3:1)*

What, then, shall we say in response to this? If God is for us, who can be against us? He who did not spare his own Son, but gave him up for us all – how will he not also, along with him, graciously give us all things? *(Romans 8:31–32)*

Suggested further reading

Ephesians 3:17–19

Reflect and respond

Identify any areas of your life that have cooled between God and you.

Look to the cross afresh, and meditate on His love for you.

38

When there Doesn't Seem any Point in *Life*

*D*o you wonder if there is any purpose to your life? Losing someone close, a change in circumstances, trauma, can all leave you wondering what the point of life is. Not just whether life is worth living, but what the point of it is now, for you.

Jeremiah 29:11 says, " *'For I know the plans I have for you,' declares the Lord, 'plans to prosper you and not to harm you, plans to give you hope and a future.'*" When things change it is important to hold onto the truth that God has a unique plan for each person's life. There is purpose and direction. Sometimes it takes time to know the plan, or to see the evidence. God promised Abraham that he would father a child. The time gap between God's promise to Abraham and Isaac's birth was 25 years! That could have been 25 years of discouragement or 25 years of faith-building.

Waiting for a vision to be fulfilled, or to see God's plan for your life, following a change, is not easy, but you need to hold onto the fact that God has a purpose.

Isaiah 42 is the first of several servant songs. It talks of God's promise concerning His servant. Though primarily talking about Jesus, we who are in Christ are also God's servants. Be encouraged by the opening words, *"Here is my servant, whom I uphold, my chosen one in whom I delight; I will put my Spirit on him and he will bring justice to the nations"* (Isaiah 42:1).

Bible Verses to Help You

"For I know the plans I have for you," declares the Lord, "plans to prosper you and not to harm you, plans to give you hope and a future." *(Jeremiah 29:11)*

And we know that in all things God works for the good of those who love him, who have been called according to his purpose. *(Romans 8:28)*

Suggested further reading
Ephesians 2:1–10

Reflect and respond
God's plans are to prosper you and to give you hope. Tell yourself this – regularly.

Rejoice that you are chosen by God.

39

When Experiencing Emptiness and *Inner Pain*

*M*uch of the emptiness which results in deep inner pain has to do with unmet needs. Human beings have different needs – identity; significance; security; self-worth. We were made to be dependent on God. Sin came in the way and the essence of sin is independence: "I can meet my own needs." The question is, where do we look for needs to be met? Usually we look either to ourselves or to others. What God says is, "Turn to me." The legacy of the Fall has to be put to death, including our attempts to meet those needs. This means wrong behaviour, ways of relating, compulsions, dependency on others, independence, etc.

When we became born again something happened! Our old nature was taken to the cross and killed. We have died with Christ and we have been buried with Him. Someone once said, "The whole point of a burial is that you say goodbye." So, we say goodbye to our identity crisis, insignificance, etc. There needs to be death and burial of the old identity so that there can be resurrection of our new identity in Christ. If you then try to meet your own needs, you are denying that God has dealt with the old.

You can let go of your own efforts and let God step in. The opposite of empty is full. What should we be filled with? The Holy Spirit. What you are full of is what you will overflow with!

Bible Verses to Help You

We were under great pressure ... But this happened that we might not rely on ourselves but on God, who raises the dead.
(2 Corinthians 1:8–9)

For you know that it was not with perishable things such as silver or gold that you were redeemed from the empty way of life handed down to you from your forefathers ...
(1 Peter 1:18)

Suggested further reading

Romans 6:1–14

Reflect and respond

Are you aware of the ache of needs in your life? God says, "Turn to me to have your needs met".

It's at the bottom we cry for help. Are you prepared to let go of your own efforts?

40

When Prompted by
Guilt

*G*uilt can be a prompting of the conscience that something is wrong in our lives, or it can be a thief that destroys our peace, resulting in insecurity and self-condemnation. There are different types of guilt: *Objective guilt* occurs when a law has been broken and we are guilty, whether we feel so or not. *Subjective guilt* is a personal feeling of discomfort, regret or remorse at having done something wrong or having failed to do something. Subjective guilt can be either true or false. *True guilt* is the feeling which occurs when we have violated a law or standard and our guilt fits our actions. *False guilt* operates from an over-sensitive conscience and does not fit our actions.

True guilt is dealt with by recognising the nature of what we have done wrong, repenting before God, asking His forgiveness, forgiving others and forgiving ourselves. Perhaps you wonder if what you have done wrong can ever be forgiven. *"If we confess our sins, he is faithful and just and will forgive us our sins and purify us from all unrighteousness*" (1 John 1:9).

When Jesus died on the cross He paid the price for every sin in the world. You confess, He forgives. False guilt can fester in our lives and cause major problems emotionally and spiritually. Resolving it involves changing our distorted thinking. Recognise that when God forgives He cancels the debt.

"The purpose of being guilty is to bring us to Jesus. Once we are there, then its purpose is finished."

Corrie Ten Boom

Bible Verses to Help You

The Sovereign Lord says: "See, I lay a stone in Zion, a tested stone, a precious cornerstone for a sure foundation; the one who trusts will never be dismayed." *(Isaiah 28:16)*

For it is by grace you have been saved, through faith – and this not from yourselves, it is the gift of God ...
(Ephesians 2:8)

Suggested further reading

Psalm 51

Reflect and respond

Have you established the type of guilt you are suffering from?

Confess your sin, receive forgiveness and rejoice in the mercy, grace and provision of God.

Do you need to put things right with others?

Content Source Material

Sections 1–5, 9 and 20–37 are taken from:
Selwyn Hughes, *Your Personal Encourager*,
CWR, 1994.

Sections 6–7 and 38–40 are taken from:
Helena Wilkinson, *Doorway to Hope*,
CWR, 1995.

Sections 8 and 10–13 are taken from:
Dr Bill & Frances Munro, *A Place of Rest*,
CWR, 1996.

Sections 14–17 are taken from:
Hilary Vogel, *Strength to Care*,
CWR, 1996.

Section 18 is taken from:
Keith Tondeur, *Facing up to Financial Crisis*,
CWR, 1995.

Section 19 is taken from:
David & Maureen Brown, *Breakthrough to Love*,
CWR, 1996.

All these titles available from CWR
(see following pages for details).

National Distributors

UK: (and countries not listed below)
CWR, PO Box 230, Farnham, Surrey GU9 8XG.
Tel: (01252) 784710 Outside UK (44) 1252 784710

AUSTRALIA: CMC Australasia, PO Box 519, Belmont, Victoria 3216.
Tel: (03) 5241 3288

CANADA: CMC Distribution Ltd, PO Box 7000, Niagara on the Lake, Ontario L0S 1J0.
Tel: (0800) 325 1297

GHANA: Challenge Enterprises of Ghana, PO Box 5723, Accra.
Tel: (021) 222437/223249 Fax: (021) 226227

HONG KONG: Cross Communications Ltd, 1/F, 562A Nathan Road, Kowloon.
Tel: 2780 1188 Fax: 2770 6229

INDIA: Crystal Communications, 10-3-18/4/1, East Marredpally, Secunderabad – 500 026.
Tel/Fax: (040) 7732801

KENYA: Keswick Bookshop, PO Box 10242, Nairobi.
Tel: (02) 331692/226047

MALAYSIA: Salvation Book Centre (M) Sdn Bhd, 23 Jalan SS 2/64, 47300 Petaling Jaya, Selangor.
Tel: (03) 78766411/78766797
Fax: (03) 78757066/78756360

NEW ZEALAND: CMC New Zealand Ltd, Private Bag, 17910 Green Lane, Auckland.
Tel: (09) 5249393 Fax: (09) 5222137

NIGERIA: FBFM, Helen Baugh House, 96 St Finbarr's College Road, Akoka, Lagos.
Tel: (01) 7747429/4700218/825775/827264

PHILIPPINES: OMF Literature Inc, 776 Boni Avenue, Mandaluyong City.
Tel: (02) 531 2183 Fax: (02) 531 1960

REPUBLIC OF IRELAND: Scripture Union, 40 Talbot Street, Dublin 1.
Tel: (01) 8363764

SINGAPORE: Campus Crusade Asia Ltd, 315 Outram Road, 06-08 Tan Boon Liat Building, Singapore 169074.
Tel: (065) 222 3640

SOUTH AFRICA: Struik Christian Books, 80 MacKenzie Street, PO Box 1144, Cape Town 8000.
Tel: (021) 462 4360 Fax: (021) 461 3612

SRI LANKA: Christombu Books, 27 Hospital Street, Colombo 1.
Tel: (01) 433142/328909

TANZANIA: CLC Christian Book Centre, PO Box 1384, Mkwepu Street, Dar es Salaam.
Tel: (051) 2119439

UGANDA: New Day Bookshop, PO Box 2021, Kampala.
Tel: (041) 255377

ZIMBABWE: Word of Life Books, Shop 4, Memorial Building, 35 S Machel Avenue, Harare.
Tel: (04) 781305 Fax: (04) 774739

For e-mail addresses, visit the CWR web site: www.cwr.org.uk

ISBN 1 85345 1789

ISBN 1 85345 1797

ISBN 1 85345 1770

ISBN 1 85345 1800

This new *Pocket Encourager* series offers biblical help, guidance and encouragement for everyone. Each title explores various aspects of the Christian experience, such as relationships, Bible study and coping with responsibility. Great gifts!

£3.99 each

Cover to Cover and *Cover to Cover – God's People* are exciting annual reading plans available in 6 partworks with their own attractive case, or as a softback book. *Cover to Cover* is now also available in hardback.

Cover to Cover

Cover to Cover explores God's Word chronologically, taking in the events of history as they happened with charts, maps, illustrations, diagrams and a helpful time line that places the Bible in a historical context.

Cover to Cover – God's People

Cover to Cover – God's People profiles 58 of the Bible's most fascinating and instructive personalities, helping you to learn invaluable lessons from these men and women of Scripture.

Softback and partworks **£9.95**

Cover to Cover hardback **£12.95**

These inspiring devotionals contain six, specially selected themes from *Every Day with Jesus* that will nourish your soul and stimulate your faith. Each book contains 365 undated daily readings, prayers, further study questions and a topical index.

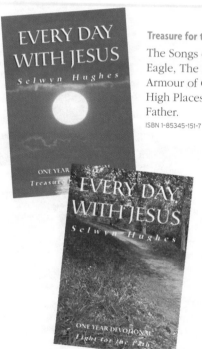

Treasure for the Heart

The Songs of Ascents, The Divine Eagle, The Lord's Prayer, The Armour of God, Hind's Feet on High Places, Your Father and My Father.

ISBN 1-85345-151-7

Light for the Path

The Uniqueness of our Faith, The Search for Meaning, The Twenty-third Psalm, The Spirit-filled Life, Strong at the Broken Places, Going Deeper with God.

ISBN 1-85345-134-7

A Fresh Vision of God

The Vision of God, From Confusion to
Confidence, The Beatitudes, The Power of a New
Perspective, The Corn of Wheat Afraid to Die,
Heaven-sent Revival.
ISBN 1-85345-121-5

Water for the Soul

Staying Spiritually Fresh,
Rebuilding Broken Walls,
The Character of God,
When Sovereignty Surprises,
The Fruit of the Spirit,
Seven Pillars of Wisdom.
ISBN 1-85345-128-2

£5.99 each

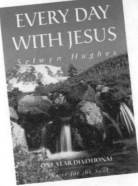

What would Christ have to say about our modern-day problems? "He would give the same answers that He gave us in His Word", says *Every Day with Jesus* author, Selwyn Hughes.

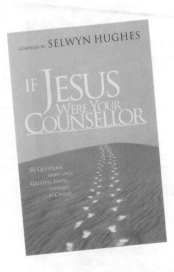

£6.95

Softback, 280 pages
198 x 130mm

If Jesus were your Counsellor offers 50 biblical answers to questions about faith and life. Selwyn Hughes brings more than four decades of counselling experience to this easy to follow and beautifully designed book, which recognises that Scripture always holds the answer.

If Jesus were your Counsellor uses *The Message* translation of the New Testament, making it contemporary and easy to understand, and the book-mark extensions to the cover provide a simple and effective way to keep your place as you read Christ's response to issues such as love, loneliness, relationships, guilt and belief.

Let Jesus be your Counsellor.

The Discipleship Series combines practical advice with biblical principles to bring you invaluable insights into your faith in Jesus and growing with Him. Each title considers some of the most vital aspects of Christian living, such as marriage, prayer, and the Church. Essential reading!

10 Principles for a Happy Marriage

- Engaging approach to marriage God's way
- Healthy marriage check list
- Practical advice and help

15 Ways to a More Effective Prayer Life

- Revolutionise your prayer life
- Flexible suggestions for the individual
- Considers different personalities and lifestyles

5 Insights to Discovering Your Place in the Body of Christ

- Understanding the gifts in Scripture
- Discovering your ministry
- Developing your gift

£3.95 each